HIERONYMUS BOSCH

MAARTEN BEKS

PARK
LANE

Cover illustrations

- The Haywain, 1500-02 (detail)
  Madrid, The Prado

- The Conjuror, 1475-80 (copy)
  Saint-Germain-en-Laye, Musée Municipal

First published in Great Britain in 1994
by Grange Books PLC
The Grange, Grange Yard, London SE1 3AG

Translated from the Dutch by Tony Langham and Plym Peters

This edition produced in co-operation with Arcturus Publishing Ltd.

Coordination and production: VBI/Smeets, Weert
Filmset: Zspiegel grafische zetterij, Best, The Netherlands
Print: Royal Smeets Offset b.v., Weert, The Netherlands

© Royal Smeets Offset b.v., Weert, The Netherlands

ISBN 1 85627 657 0

HIERONYMUS BOSCH

Hieronymus (Jheronimus, Jeroen van Aken) was probably born in 1453 in 's-Hertogenbosch, where he died in August 1516.

Although Hieronymus Bosch was one of the most famous painters of the late Middle Ages, very little is known about his life. He worked in the city of his birth all his life, but his fame spread far beyond this prosperous, though in cultural terms, rather isolated town. The fact that he enjoyed an international reputation is clear from the prestigious commissions he received: in 1504, Philip the Fair commissioned a triptych of the Last Judgement. At approximately the age of twenty-four, Jeroen Bosch married Aeleyt van de Meervenne, a girl with a patrician background. As a result of his marriage he acquired estates in the neighbourhood of Oirschot in 1484. Two years later, he was registered as a member of the local Illustrious Fraternity of Our Lady, better known as the Swan Fraternity.

Bosch's imagination was closely related to the spiritual climate of his time. Epidemics of the plague, spiritual confusion, witchcraft, the persecution of heretics, and social upheaval all left traces in his otherworldly landscapes. In addition to being a visionary, he was a moralist with a pessimistic view of mankind, and he saw man as being characterized by folly, with an inclination towards evil, on his way to hell.

There is no information to show that Bosch had pupils, but it is clear that his work was diligently copied throughout the sixteenth century, and that an army of successors mastered the heritage he left them. After the sixteenth century, the interest in Hieronymus Bosch waned. His work was rediscovered only towards the end of the nineteenth century. The Symbolists and Surrealists respected him as their most important precursor.

The Hearing Wood and Seeing Field, Pen and ink drawing

HIERONYMUS BOSCH

Hieronymus Bosch is an unknown man, whose name is linked to a number of famous paintings. We know hardly anything about his life. There are no letters, no diaries, no anecdotes, and hardly any official documents. His work can be interpreted in many different ways, but cannot be read as a biography.

What is known about him is not much more than the information usually given in a passport. The lives of countless forgotten artists were better recorded than his. Great men owned his works - Philip the Fair, Margaret of Austria, Cardinal Grimani, Philip II - but the records of his life were no more memorable than those of all the others who shared his family name, Van Aken, who were also registered as painters in the guild's archives of the city of 's-Hertogenbosch. Even the meticulous Karel van Mander barely managed to fill in any detail in his *Schilderboeck*. He too described only the works produced by Bosch's illustrious brush, but had nothing to say about the man himself. So there is little more than the portrait of a solid and anonymous shopkeeper. Did Jheronimus van Aken, who called himself Bosch, assume a different name to establish his artistic personality and distinguish himself from the dynasty of Van Akens, who were respected craftsmen ? Edward Cohen, who wrote an original book about Bosch, suggested this. But although "Jeroen de Maelre" is entered in the archives of the "Illustrious Fraternity of Our Lady" in Den Bosch as a "very celebrated artist", his personality disappears completely behind his profession. His biography is such a blank sheet that any assumptions can be defended with equal conviction. Did he go on a long journey to present a triptych to Philip the Fair personally ? Did he travel to Italy around the turn of the century during a period about which absolutely nothing is known, and did he come across (the work of) Leonardo da Vinci during his time in the south, so that certain changes in the style of his work could be attributed to Leonardo's influence ? In short, the assumptions made about Jeroen are similar to those made about Johannes Vermeer of Delft, who is also hidden behind his paintings.

It may be of interest to examine Jheronimus Bosch's certificate of baptism, if only to show even more clearly that his "curriculum vitae" is extremely sketchy, compared with everything that is known about others who have been totally forgotten. Hieronymus or Jheronimus van Aken was born in Den Bosch in 1453, the son of the painter, Anthonis van Aken. At the age of twenty-four, he married Aeleyt van der Meerveene, the daughter of a distinguished family; it was a marriage above his station. She brought him some estates, and consequently Hieronymus was able to afford to live a quiet life behind his easel. In 1486, he was registered as a member of the Illustrious Fraternity of Our Lady, which was founded in 1328, probably because he had become an important figure, as well as "celebrated", as a result of his marriage. This fraternity was aimed at promoting devotion to the Mother of God and dispensing charity. Documents relating to all sorts of transactions show that the world knew about his exceptional talents, and that the city of his birth also honoured him with important commissions. He died in 1516. Because his wife belonged to a distinguished family, there is almost more in the archives about her than about her famous husband.

Thanks to the patient research of the archives by J. Mosmans and Father Gerlach, amongst others, we at least know where he lived: on the Grote Markt. The Noordbrabants Museum in Den Bosch owns an anonymous painting in which Bosch's house can be identified. This tells us little more about the master. However, it is clear that he was an important man who cared more about his social reputation than international fame.

It is clear from the name which he chose that Bosch was proud of the city of his birth, where he lived separately from the art world. Den Bosch was certainly more than "a marsh with a cathedral and a few houses around it", as Alphons Diepenbrock tried to convince his friends in Amsterdam more than four hundred years later.

Probably it was quite a lot more peaceful, as well as more boring, than the capitals on the map of European art. However, safety was a great virtue in those great, though grim times. The dates which mark Bosch's life are easy to remember, even for those who forget all dates. The year of his birth, 1453, saw the downfall of the Holy Roman Empire in the east - how did Bosch hear about that ? - and the year of his death, 1516, saw the arrival of Luther.

During his lifetime, America was discovered, and apart from Columbus and numerous other great discoverers, his contemporaries include Gutenberg and Laurens Jansz. Coster, the great founders of the first information explosion, and therefore Luther's most important allies. The appearance of the world changed, and changes also took place in Den Bosch, for it was by no means the least important of the cities of the Burgundian empire, which was on the point of disintegrating. The great disaster, the Eighty Years' War, was still some way off, but everything which made the waning of the Middle Ages such a dreadful time - the persecution of heretics, witchcraft and witches - was present throughout the Empire, and certainly in the Grote Markt in Den Bosch.

This waning, which was experienced as a revival in Italy, and put a definite end to the disconsolate medieval winter, brought endless disasters - superstition and intolerance - which had never existed in the Middle Ages. Many enlightened minds, who were forerunners of independent Renaissance thinking, including such famous figures as Melanchton, Sir William Harvey and Lope de Vega, but probably also Hieronymus Bosch, considered sorcery and witchcraft as a real danger, and believed that its eradication with the well-known repugnant means, to be the sacred duty of the Church and the secular authorities. The great rulers who succeeded the medieval feudal lords promoted the safety of the majority as powerfully as the unsafe plight of the numerous minorities, because their realms no longer had any boundaries which could be passed by refugees. Unlike in Italy, where an interesting refugee could usually find protection with one tyrant against the arbitrary tyranny of another important "gangster", there was hardly any safe haven in the north for anyone who had fallen into disrepute.

A GREAT AGE, BUT WHO WOULD WANT TO HAVE LIVED THEN ?

Rudy Kousbroek raised this familiar question in his introduction to a book about Leonardo's inventions. Leonardo was born a year before Bosch and died two years after him (1452-1590). How does someone who is left behind by rebellious astronauts on a journey through time, behave in Den Bosch in the fifteenth century ? Most problems which arise in this situation are as fascinating as they are insoluble. But there is only one answer to the question about how someone in that position would feel - they would feel dreadful. Any time other than one's own time is a prison, but in our imagination the fifteenth and sixteenth centuries have the character of a world-encompassing dungeon. Therefore it is not really very surprising that someone with Bosch's awesome imagination did all he could to lead a retiring life. In fact, his contemporaries were strongly advised to do so by the companions of Geert Grote, the "Brothers of the Community of Life", who were very influential in Den Bosch. Another interesting question which arises is whether someone who was deposited in the fifteenth century could have developed to become a painter of Bosch's stature, because he was ahead of his time. But what exactly do we mean when we say that Bosch was ahead of his time ? In fact, we do not really mean anything by it, because only the fifteenth century, a time of discoveries and great physical and metaphysical fear, fits Bosch the artist like a glove.

According to Kousbroek and other authors who abandoned the romantic view of genius, this also applies to Leonardo da Vinci, although it should be established immediately that Leonardo was a father of the future, and Bosch was in many respects a child of the past. As a provincial genius - for there was hardly any artistic tradition in Den Bosch - he trailed behind the procession led by Leonardo da Vinci in the history of art. What Leonardo saw as the beginning of an era of rationality, and of a new sense of realism, was for Bosch the beginning of the end, degeneracy, and the decay of truth and values. His voyages of discovery always resulted in even more accurately charted images of horror. The austere Philip II admired his work, which confirmed his fears, and which he probably saw as a justification for his own measures to expand his reign of terror. Leonardo was fairly indifferent with regard to Church dogma, and was probably too much concerned with problems of a scientific nature to be identified as a true believer or arch heretic. Bosch was more likely to have become a heretic, despite everything, if he had not happened to have been a painter, and was therefore himself a disseminator of the worst of the vanities, i.e., culture.

Perhaps we should interpret the paintings of Hieronymus Bosch as a great judgement of heresy, in which only a madman - in his case, acting in the guise of a Spanish Dominican - was able to discover heresy, but another possibility should be allowed for: that Bosch actually was a heretic, and that he expressed his heresy - which will be explained below - in a secret code which was totally comprehensible to other initiates, but told a completely different and familiar story to other outsiders. Did Bosch's message have a secret character, or was it also meant for those who were not initiated ? Was official Church dogma his subject, or a cloak for his real subject matter ?

HERETIC OR A PERSECUTOR OF HERETICS ?

Was Bosch a heretic, or did he persecute heretics ? This controversy dominated the interpretation of Bosch's work for several decades and divided his admirers into two embittered camps. The conflict was introduced in a brilliant book documented in great detail by Wilhelm Fraenger. Fraenger built a glittering tower - though it floated a few centimetres above the ground - because the foundation stone of the structure was at roof level.

It was never proved that Bosch was a member of a heretical sect which had a liturgy based on strange sexual rituals, because no evidence has been found which proves the existence of this sect in Den Bosch. However, this book could explain a great deal about many of the things which remain obscure in orthodox explanations, or have been left out of consideration altogether. Consequently it convinced many famous scholars. According to Charles de Tolnay, the methods of in-depth psychology and modern sociology were often applied in a fascinating, though generally arbitrary way "in Fraenger's excellently written analysis". Although Fraenger's writings contain interesting detailed observations, he reduces Bosch's personality in its totality to a passive interpreter of the ideas of Jacob van Almaengien (the heretic king), his alleged patron, and consequently insufficient credit is given to the master's creative originality. This criticism seems rather forced, as though De Tolnay is doing his best to maintain his lack of faith vis-à-vis his learned colleagues. As usual, his declaration has the effect of making his views even less credible. De Tolnay notes that Fraenger applied research methods which touched upon the structure of the artistic imagination, unlike most other methods. However, subsequently he withdrew this compliment, without any support for the argument that these methods were used "arbitrarily". This in itself sounds rather arbitrary. Why should Fraenger's theory reduce Bosch to a "passive interpreter" of someone else's ideas, and yet give him full credit if he were seen as an interpreter of the true faith? Is an explanation which identifies every monstrous creature, every terrifying hellish situation, as a visual translation of a popular proverb or saying, less critical of Bosch as an artist than an interpretation which sees him as an inventor of symbols which can be interpreted in (at least) two ways?

In other words: the attempt to find the right interpretation of Bosch's own language in itself has become a conflict between orthodox and heretical views, between scientific faith and heresy which was considered unscientific. In fact, De Tolnay was aware that during this holy war between Bosch experts, the painter Bosch completely disappeared from sight. All the discussions which took place about his work could be held, possibly with even more justification, about the work of an artist who was completely unimportant from the artistic point of view. Poor and extremely mediocre artists are more representative of their time than artists who are recognized by succeeding generations as being the best of their time. A good artist provides us with the image which he formed of his own time, while a mediocre artist faithfully interprets the ideas of the century which produces them. If we succeed in reading Hieronymus Bosch as his contemporaries wished to understand him, we have obtained some useful information about Bosch's period, but this does not in any way explain why we are so intrigued and fascinated by Bosch, the unreadable artist, and why, following a long period of oblivion, he was discovered at the end of the nineteenth century as one of the great fifteenth century masters of the northern Netherlands. One may well wonder why twentieth century artists are interested in Hieronymus Bosch.

Edward Cohen makes a distinction in the literature on Bosch between knowledge and ignorance of this artist. He classified the daring statements of characters such as Fraenger as ignorance about Bosch because they lack the argument to convince the experts, though they do pay tribute to his artistry and imagination. Those ignorant about Bosch, like the artists who have discovered Bosch, see symbols where the experts on Bosch recognize puzzles, which can be solved with a knowledge of proverbs, theology and folklore. Obviously these analysts carry out extremely important historical work, but because no one thought about the strength of Bosch's own arguments while they were giving their explanation, Bosch was in danger of becoming proverbially boring in the eyes of his ignorant admirers, the hobby horse of specialists and the horror of all those who are afraid of art without footnotes.

Those who were ignorant about Bosch understood him before he was explained by the experts, just as many seventeenth century still lifes and genre painters were understood before anyone had explained the references to the Bible, to the work of Jacob Cats or to a book of symbols, at the only level where they were meaningful. It is all very well to know this, but completely useless when it concerns the question whether Hieronymus Bosch, Jan Steen or Adriaan Brouwer deserve a permanent place in museums.

The fact that artists in this century have frequently turned away from Bosch is undoubtedly related to this tendency of experts to identify Bosch's paintings with their historical background, never raising the question why this artist, in contrast with countless other nameless but diligent colleagues, succeeded in producing art "in a popular language", and in forging symbols from material which remained what it was in others' hands: symbols without any added value. Art is a way of embodying meaning. Bosch's commentators have narrowed this meaning down to a conventional meaning by analyzing it in a way in which robs the work of the life of an artistic language.

The commentators on Pieter Bruegel the Elder never succeeded in doing this. How can this be explained? In this context, one should remember that experts on Bruegel, as well as those who are ignorant of his art, are convinced that Bruegel was a (much) greater artist than Hieronymus Bosch.

They also thought that one of the characteristics of Bosch's work which has nothing to do with quality is that Bosch's paintings should be viewed from close up. Therefore, the paintings became particularly popular with near-sighted people who could no longer see the wood, i.e., Bosch, for the trees. While Bruegel keeps us - and even the critics with the magnifying glasses - at a distance, Bosch created a sense of constriction, whilst Bruegel, even when he depicted horrors, made room for a look at the good earth to show happiness. The landscape as a delight and restful sight for the eye is always revealed in Bosch's work as a detail, against the oppression of hellish and heavenly forces, and can usually be enjoyed after the eye has turned away from all these depressing matters. Very often, books on art explain these small motifs more clearly than a look at the paintings themselves. Bosch painted magnificent landscapes, but it is as though he consciously concealed them because the prospect of the next life should always have the upper hand over the view of this life. Sometimes Bosch also painted the landscape as though viewed through a keyhole, as a prospect of something - compassion - which cannot be lost even in the darkest night.

Bosch was undoubtedly familiar with the magical illuminated books by the Limberg brothers and those of many others who "discovered" the landscape, and in this way laid the foundation for a world of mysticism in which the spiritual and physical eye could ultimately come together. Because of their discovery, the world became "externalized inner reality" and - according to the views of the romantic philosopher Schilling, the mind became an "internalized reality", and the human eye finally acquired its "human rights" (Aby Warburg).

It looks as though Bosch found it difficult to accept these "human rights of the eye" and that he saw the landscape as something permitted insofar as it gave a view of a corner of paradise from a world overrun with the flowers of evil, in which it is really always night.

Bosch's early work is more modern than anything created after the turn of the century, insofar as it expresses a more harmonious relationship with the manifestations of the visible world. That is why it is almost impossible to imagine that the "more mature" period after 1500 was introduced by a trip to Italy, as many experts have suggested. One would rather imagine a different adventure, a trip to the end of the night, and therefore to an underground realm inhabited by monsters whose supreme power can only be undone by the senses. Night has fallen, the obsessions of darkness have this kingdom to themselves and not so much as a memory remains of the brightness of day. The soul has lost its belief in the eye and in visible reality.

A JOURNEY THROUGH THE NIGHT OF THE SOUL

Salvador Dali, a late follower of Hieronymus Bosch said of his own work that it was the result of a systematic staged paranoia: he scrutinized everything close on the heels of someone leaving the realm of light and of sensory perception. As he flees, the artist "photographs" all the faces of fear. What De Tolnay called "the separation from the world" is also a conscious turning away from the day and from the beauty of the world, and therefore at the same time a fascination with the world of the night and its phantoms. This smacks of heresy, as traditional evening prayers warn us in so many words. Landscape artists saw reality as a vision. Bosch sacrificed reality to the vision, and sensory information to the monsters which are produced by the spirit during sleep.

Hieronymus's journey through "the night of the soul" (as described by Saint John of the Cross) also has an element of the systematic examination of a forbidden area which was viewed with great suspicion by the Church. Therefore, it is quite conceivable that Bosch tried to legitimize this forbidden journey by translating the unknown language spoken there into the safe language of proverbs, folklore, stories about "The pilgrim's journey" and popular variations of Dante's journey through hell, such as "The Vision of Tondalus", which is not dangerous. The well-known symbols used in Bosch's visions seem more like the packaging, the cloaks of love which are aimed at concealing the true symbols from the view of simple believers and short-sighted inquisitors. The adaptation in retrospect of the unmentionable to the more or less mentionable - the symbol in its symbolic language - is strongly reminiscent of what has been known as "the censorship of dreams" ever since Freud. Unlike Surrealist artists, fifteenth and sixteenth century artists endeavoured to keep their obsessions under control. They were still ashamed of insanity and absurdity, and did not think there was a place for these: in the world of temptations - "The Temptation of Saint Anthony" - by the demons which should be kept in control while the artist was painting. After all, despairing of salvation from this darkness is the "unforgivable sin", and immediately led to a suspicion of heresy. The Manicheanism which rejects nature as being completely depraved is always lying in wait, and in his later works Bosch ventured dangerously close to the abyss: disassociating oneself from the world could result in a denial of the world. However, dogma insisted that the world was saved and the theology of Thomas of Aquinus, influenced by Aristotle, opted for the belief in the reality of the world which was created by God, and not by the Devil. The question arises whether Bosch could have defended himself against the accusation of heresy if the most powerful figures of his time had not granted him safe conduct. Perhaps the heresy of Hieronymus Bosch was only legitimised by a Spanish heresy exercised by the King of Spain. But perhaps what we see as "heresy" is mainly an expression of provincialism. In this context, it is appropriate to quote a sentence from a particularly good essay by Lambert Tegenbosch: "What Bosch does, he does with the headstrong character of the provincial figure: the only time that he was valued outside 's-Hertogenbosch, in sixteenth century Spain, Bosch ("boscesca") was synonymous with mad. The Spaniards themselves were provincial and mad enough to value another provincial madman who transcended them in this respect, led in this by their king".

In 1925, the occultist, Fulcanelli, of whose life nothing else is known, published an extremely strange book entitled "Le Mystère des Cathédrales". He defended the view that the sculptures in medieval cathedrals can be seen as an encyclopedia of the secret science of alchemy. Obviously he distinguished a superficial and more profound meaning aimed respectively at the profane, who recognized the well-known Biblical and legendary tales in them, and at the initiated, to whom the key of the code was revealed. This secret science, called the "Kabbala" by Fulcanelli, was heretical in the eyes of the Church because the Church considered the events related in the Gospels as representing a message which was, in principle, comprehensible to everyone. The Church had early on rejected the elite form of Christianity, intended only for those "with ears to hear and eyes to see", which, moreover, views the Book of Revelations as pre-Christian wisdom (gnosis). However, according to the occultists, this wisdom survived in underground sects who were forced to communicate with each other in a secret language.

Fraenger's notorious book in a sense elaborated on the writings of Fulcanelli. The difference between Fulcanelli and Fraenger is, above all, that in relation to Bosch, Fraenger does not think so much in terms of a secret language, but of a transformation of heretical ideas into traditional Church language under the influence of unconscious adaptation mechanisms. The formless elements are translated into "archetypes" (primitive images of the collective unconscious), which in their turn were also subject to censorship: the scope of the "Self" corrected the manifestations of the other sphere. This means that Bosch did not have to violate his art in order to make his heretical message generally comprehensible and acceptable, also because ambiguity was an essential aspect of the symbols.

Therefore it is not particularly important to know what Bosch himself meant. Would we stop admiring him if we discovered that he merely intended to teach us? Bosch's night, everything which cannot be distinguished in the dark, is much more frightening than all the things which can be seen in detail in those sad processions and carnival parades of devils and damned souls. This can be put another way: Hieronymus Bosch did not paint a dictionary of alchemy, but his painting depicts an alchemical process.

THE UNKNOWN ALCHEMIST

"In the 'Aurora consurgens' the unknown alchemist summons the king's son who lives in the dark depths of the sea. This prince of exile has settled in the muddy depths and his soul cannot be reached by natural means. He sighs in the heart of the sombre ocean, but he also sighs in each of us, because this radiant and immortal flame lives in the darkness of our souls and is an unknown doppelganger whose laments can only penetrate occasionally through the masks of the nightmare. Bosch's work invites us to jump into that ocean. In this life about which history tells us hardly anything, every painting and every drawing is like a stage of a long sea journey which comes to an end only when it has reached its predestined shore, where we will be received as royal sons and children of the sun". These are the opening words of a curious book, "Jérome Bosch", by Claude Mettra.

It is also possible to write about Bosch from the unprovable conviction that Bosch was a hermit who exclusively devoted himself to completing the "Magnus Opus", the "Great Work" as "the unknown alchemist". This was not concerned with making gold, but with the metamorphosis of the soul and body into an ephemeral matter and deification. The realization that Bosch included a great deal of alchemy and astrology in his imagery as well as many proverbs and generally accessible wisdom, is currently widespread in the books which are included in the serious literature on Bosch. The question arises, of course, whether Bosch merely added alchemical and astrological terms and attributes to the imagery of his idiom, or whether he viewed painting itself as a secret science with techniques that corresponded in many ways to the secret science of alchemy. There was a third possibility: that the invention of painting in oils was the result of an alchemical experiment, and actually the only result which survived the centuries and the arrival of systematic chemistry.

Therefore, the question should actually be formulated as follows: was alchemy merely another means of expression for Bosch or was it a dominant theme of painting itself? Anyone who chooses the latter possibility will find that this theory is very popular with contemporary artists who devote themselves in their work above all to rethinking the invention of painting in oils.

What mysterious process takes place in the closed circuit of brain, hand, a medium (paint) and the canvas which is covered with paint. How can this "mud", reveal the "royal son", "our unknown doppelganger", if the process is carried out properly? In alchemy, this may have taken place in a metaphorical sense; in painting, the process took place in a way which could be controlled by anyone: the marriage of spirit and matter resulted in a world which had not been "created". The painting became a screen on which dreams were projected which looked very different from the inner images which the painter had wished to project. The artist discovered that he was clairvoyant when he painted, while he was by no means a visionary when he did not paint.

In traditional aesthetics, art is "a form of successful expression": the artist is successful if he has said what he wanted to say. However, every artist knows that the image which ultimately emerges in the painting is not the same as his original intention, and he would be the first to agree that this cannot always be considered a "loss". In fact, the painter aims to profit from the situation, for the painting should give him back more than it has received from him. The alchemists must have been familiar with this experience: the alchemical wedding created new life; it was not a reproduction of existing life. The painting is fertilized. There is no question of production in a technical sense, because this can never bring about mutations in man's designs by its own strength.

The modern view of art is loaded with alchemical imagery. Perhaps it is conceivable that the first generations of artists who discovered that they had not entirely mastered their artistic endeavours, and could therefore perform magic, saw this occult terminology in a completely literal sense. Perhaps they did view the painting as a mysterious optical instrument, a mirror which did not reflect their familiar "Self", but the known face of the doppelganger. When Bosch is described as the great painter of mystery, this probably refers above all to a painter who celebrated the mystery of painting.

THE REDISCOVERY OF HIERONYMUS BOSCH

In support of this view, it may be appropriate to remember that Hieronymus Bosch, who had been totally forgotten, was rediscovered in the nineteenth century not by scholars, but by artists. It was the fin-de-siècle Symbolists who saved this genius from provincial museums. They discovered the clairvoyance of this artist who had been considered small-minded and superstitious, and presented the Surrealists of this century with their strongest historical argument.

At the end of 1985, the Noordbrabants Museum in Bosch's own city exhibited a number of works by contemporary visual artists who had responded to the invitation to complete, as they saw fit, the famous triptych of The Flood in Rotterdam, the central panel of which is missing. It became clear that the artists were not particularly interested in Hieronymus Bosch as a painter of hell, and that many had overcome their initial revulsion when they had studied Bosch's artistic method, insofar as this can be reduced to art as a secret science. Bosch did not invent things, his images of horror appeared of their own accord. Many entries to the exhibition tried to re-enact this self-realization of the painting under the protective hands of the painter - the gardener looking after his garden.

They sought a method which would show that the subject of the central panel cannot be looked for, but must be simply found, in the same way that Bosch had discovered the trail.

As long as artists attribute the monopoly on this occult technique to Hieronymus Bosch, unravelling this science will be an exciting thing to do. However, as soon as explanations manage to obscure the paintings - as they almost have in the last few decades - art should remind science once again that Hieronymus Bosch did not paint proverbs, but paintings.

The Ship of Fools, 1485-1505
Panel, 58 x 32.5 cm
Paris, The Louvre

The dating is very inexact
(1485/90-1505), but this
painting is generally
considered to be a work
from Bosch's first period.
Perhaps it was originally
part of a cycle of
representations of all sorts
of forbidden sensual
delights (the rest of which
have not survived). Bosch
probably based it on a
book by Sebastiaan Brant,
"Das Narrenschiff"
(The Ship of Fools).

Left: The Haywain, 1500-02
Middle panel of a triptych, 136 x 100 cm
Madrid, The Prado

The Haywain, detail from the middle panel

"The world is a haywain; everybody grabs what he can get."
(Flemish proverb, quoted on an engraving by Bartholomeus de Momper, after Bosch.)

The Garden of Earthly Delights, 1503-04
Panel, (closed), 220 x 195 cm
Creation of the World
Madrid, The Prado

Paradise
Left-hand panel of The Haywain, 136 x 48 cm

Hell
Right-hand panel of The Haywain, 136 x 48 cm

The outer panels provide an other-worldly perspective on the human virtues and vices depicted in the middle panel

The Garden of Earthly Delights, 1503-04, middle panel of a triptych, 220 x 197 cm, Madrid, The Prado

An apotheosis of ambiguity, but going up the three levels of this painting which is composed in layers, it becomes increasingly clear what motivates the courtly figures in the foreground, who interact so elegantly and distantly. The proper forms are an introduction to - and postponement of - the wild circuit of desire which is shown in the central area. The realm of the unnatural starts at the top.

rden of Earthly Delights, detail of the middle panel

Paradise (Garden of Eden)
Left-hand panel of the Garden of Earthly Delights,
220 x 97 cm
Madrid, The Prado

The world is completely serene, but there are
literally serpents under the grass. Adam sees Eve
"with other eyes", and that is the beginning of
the chaos which is depicted on the middle panel.

Paradise
Detail of the left-hand panel

When sensuality has stolen into paradise,
animals start to prey on each other.
The lion no longer sleeps with the lamb.

The Musical Hell
Right-hand panel of the Garden of Earthly Delights,
220 x 97 cm
Madrid, The Prado

Human figures are attached to or intertwined
with musical instruments which originally
caressed their ears and then enticed them to
fornication.

The Musical Hell
Detail of the right-hand panel

27

The Musical Hell
Detail of the right-hand panel

The suffering of sensuality

The Musical Hell
Detail of the right-hand panel

The Conjuror (copy)
Panel, 53 x 65 cm
Saint-Germain-en-Laye, Municipal Museum

The crowd watches breathlessly as a conjuror produces a frog from the mouth of an observer, so that no one notices the pickpocket.

The Conjuror, detail

The Prodigal Son, 1510
Panel, diameter 64.6
Rotterdam, Boymans -
van Beuningen Museum

Everything in this painting is characterized by the choice between good and evil, left and right. Back to his father's estate and/or to the brothel, with the sign of the white swan. The end remains undecided, although believers know better.

The Prodigal Son, detail

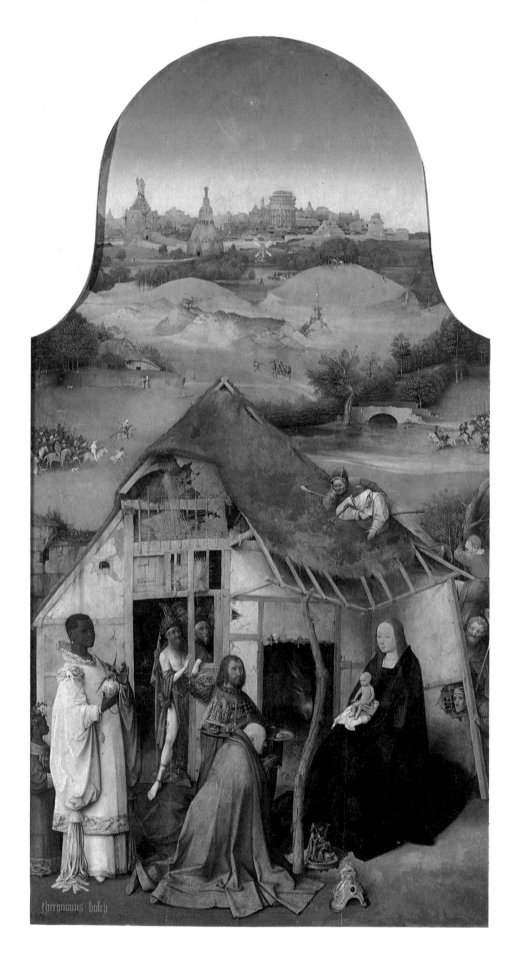

The Adoration of the Kings
(Epiphany Triptych)
Middle panel of a triptych
138 x 72 cm
Madrid, The Prado

Even the Adoration of the
Kings, usually represented in
those days as a rustic idyll
which appeals directly to the
heart, serves as a vehicle for
Bosch's theological views,
brimming with references
which cannot be identified
with any certainty. Who are
the figures in the stable ?
Are they prophets from
the Old Testament, the
Antichrist and his followers,
or possibly Herod and his
henchmen ? De Tolnay
interprets this painting as an
allegory of the Holy Mass
sacrifice: Mary as a living
altar, the Three Kings as
priests.

The Donor with St. Peter
and St. Joseph
Left-hand panel of The
Adoration of the Kings
138 x 33 cm

The Donor with St. Agnes
Right-hand panel of The
Adoration of the Kings
138 x 33 cm

The Birth of Christ
c. 1508
Panel, 105 x 84 cm
Cologne, Wallraf-Richartz
Museum

Some critics believe that
this painting is a copy;
in fact, there are two
known versions.

The Adoration of the Three
Kings, 1480-85
Panel, 74 x 54 cm
Philadelphia, Museum of Art
The John G. Johnson Collection

The Wedding Feast at Cana
Panel, 93 x 72 cm
Rotterdam, Boymans - van Beuningen Museum

The Wedding Feast at Cana, detail

Is this another allegory of the Eucharist ? Does Bosch wish to show that all those who are present are heretics (as De Tolnay maintains) ? It is difficult to support this view while at the same time maintaining that Bosch intended to relate the Wedding Feast at Cana to the annual swan meal of the Illustrious Fraternity Of Our Lady in Den Bosch, of which Bosch was a member. The swan is carried in, as well as a boar's head. Perhaps this is a reference after all to the presence of true believers, as well as heretics, in this company.

Ecce Homo, panel, 75 x 61 cm
Frankfurt, Städelsches Kunstinstitut

Ecce Homo, detail

Christ Crowned with Thorns, 1508-09
Panel, 73 x 59 cm
London, The National Gallery

The caricatured representation of the bystanders has
given rise to a political interpretation of this painting:
could these thugs be meant to represent the powerful
figures who emerged following the division of the
Burgundian empire as a result of the death of
Charles the Bold ?

Christ Crowned with Thorns, c. 1510
Panel, 165 x 195 cm
Madrid, El Escorial

N.B. the grisaille painting outside
the circle, showing the fall of the
angels.

Christ Carrying the Cross, 1515-1516
Panel, 74 x 81 cm
Ghent, Museum of Fine Arts

De Tolnay has suggested that Bosch was
influenced by Leonardo da Vinci with regard
to the caricatured features of the bystanders.
This influence supposedly made itself felt
during Bosch's alleged trip to Italy.

Christ Carrying the Cross, detail

St. Christopher, 1504-05, panel, 113 x 71.5 cm
Rotterdam, Boymans - van Beuningen Museum

John the Baptist in
the Wilderness, 1504-05
Panel, 48.5 x 40 cm
Madrid, Lazaro Galdiano Museum

The landscape is partly peaceful and partly
covered with unnatural vegetation. The world of
hallucination, fear, and sensual images appears
between reality and vision.

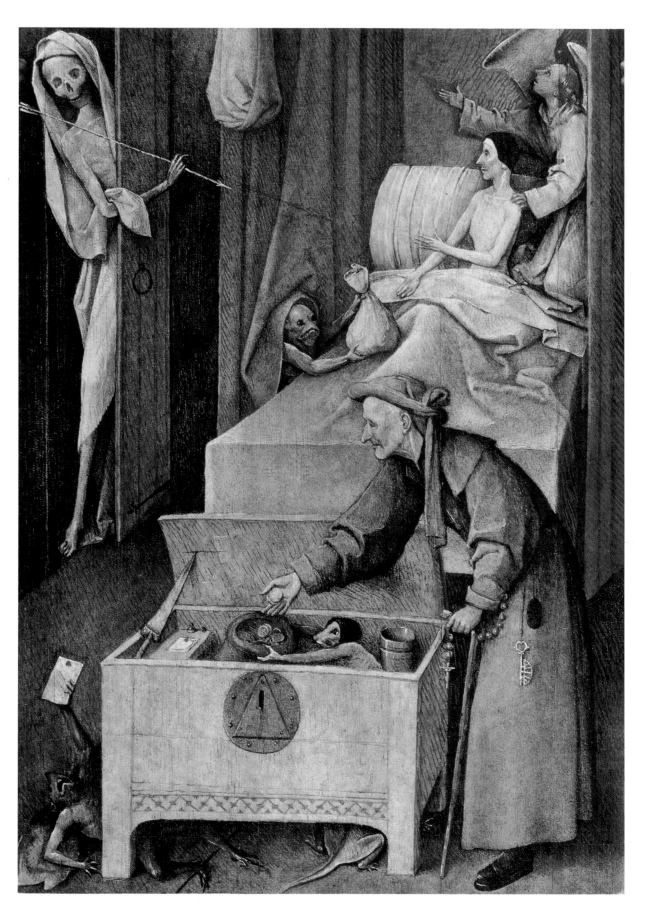

Death of the Miser, detail, c. 1490, panel, complete painting 93 x 31 cm,
Washington D.C., National Gallery of Art, Samuel H. Kress Collection

The legend: Julia, a virgin of patrician descent, was sold to a heathen Syrian merchant, Eusebius, as a slave. On his travels while trading, Eusebius, accompanied by Julia, landed in Corsica to make a sacrifice to the gods. She remained behind on the beach, where she attracted the attention of the governor of the island. He tried to gain her favours, but his attempts were in vain, and he forcefully abducted her. When she refused to make a sacrifice to the gods, she was crucified.

The Crucifixion of St. Julia, before 1505
Middle panel of the triptych
The Martyrdom of St. Julia,
104 x 63 cm
Venice, Ducal Palace

49

The Temptation of St. Anthony
Middle panel of the St. Anthony triptych
131.5 x 119 cm
Lisbon, Museu Nacional de Arte Antiga

The witches' sabbath. St. Anthony in the grip
of the forces of darkness. Bosch possessed by
a delusion of witches.

The Temptation of
St. Anthony
Detail of the middle panel

Bottom right-hand corner:
a devilish priest reads
the Black Mass.

The Evil Torture, 1505-06
Left-hand panel of the triptych
The Temptation of
St. Anthony
131.5 x 53 cm
Lisbon, Museu Nacional
de Arte Antiga

The forces of hell use every
means, hard and soft, to turn
St. Anthony's gaze, which he
has turned away from the
world, towards the illusory
figures of evil.

The Temptation
Right-hand panel of the
triptych of The Temptation
of St. Anthony
131.5 x 53 cm

St. Anthony caught
between two temptations:
in front of him there is
a tempting woman who
proffers herself from
behind a ghostly, rootless
tree, and next to him there
is a table carried by sensual
demons.

The Last Judgement, middle panel of a triptych, 163.7 x 127 cm
Vienna, Galerie der Akademie der Bildenden Künste

Hell, right-hand panel of
The Last Judgement triptych,
167.7 x 60 cm

Paradise, left-hand panel of
The Last Judgement triptych,
167.7 x 60 cm

Fragment of a Last Judgement, detail, panel, complete painting 60 x 114 cm
Munich, Alte Pinakothek